D1710086

The Shaman
and the
Water Serpent

The Shaman and the Water Serpent

Jennifer Owings Dewey

Illustrations by Benton Yazzie

UNIVERSITY OF NEW MEXICO PRESS
ALBUQUERQUE

© 2007 by the University of New Mexico Press
All rights reserved. Published 2007
Printed and bound in China through Four Colour Imports, Ltd.

YEAR							PRINTING						
13	12	11	10	09	08	07	1	2	3	4	5	6	7

Library of Congress Cataloging-in-Publication Data

Dewey, Jennifer.
  The shaman and the water serpent / Jennifer Owings Dewey ; illustrations by Benton Yazzie.
     p. cm.
  ISBN-13: 978-0-8263-4211-9 (cloth : alk. paper)
  1. Pueblo Indians—Folklore. 2. Animals—Folklore. 3. Rock paintings—Southwest, New—Juvenile literature.
4. Petroglyphs—Southwest, New—Juvenile literature. 5. Southwest, New—Antiquities—Juvenile literature.
I. Yazzie, Benton, 1972– ill. II. Title.
  E99.P9D37 2007
  979'.01—dc22
                                        2006023545

Cover illustration by Jennifer Owings Dewey

Book design and composition by Damien Shay
Body type is Garamond 20/28
Display is Caslon Antique and Adobe Caslon

Introduction

Men, women, and children pecked and painted pictures on stones thousands of years ago and today we look at these pictures and wonder about them. What did they mean to the people who made them?

The Puebloans, as they are named, lived close to the Earth and knew well the butterflies, lizards, snakes, birds, antelope, and other animals living all around them. They knew the habits of these animals and hunted many of them for food. Instead of writing stories on paper—there was no paper then—they told stories about their surroundings, using voices and gesturing with their hands. They also preserved stories for all time by making images on stones.

Then, as now, people marked the seasons with celebrations and ceremonies. Sometimes a ceremony or a ritual called for making a picture on stone. Other times the picture was made to show where water was, or to celebrate the sighting of many deer, or perhaps to mark a shooting star streaking across the night sky.

This book tells a story, too, and here the story is made partly with words, partly with pictures, so people of today can get an idea of how those ancient Puebloans lived their lives.

The Shaman

In some ancient cultures the shaman was a man or woman with supernatural power. The shaman offered the People insight into the mysterious world of gods and spirits. The weather, illness, and evil were all controlled by the shaman. Because the shaman was able to speak to the spirits, partly through the pictures he or she made on rock surfaces, the animal spirits were coaxed into making hunts successful and insuring the return of rain after a dry spell.

The Water Serpent

People of long ago associated the snake with water and rain. The snake moves along the ground as water travels between the banks of a river: curving and winding. The way a snake moves also brings to mind the lightning that accompanies a thunderstorm.

Because snakes live in dens below the surface of the Earth where there are springs of fresh water, snakes were in control of water sources. The People danced to the snake and drew its image on rocks to implore it to bring back the rain after the dry season.

Our world is made of fire,
water, soil, and air.

The wind blows and we feel it on our faces,
but we never see it.

We are the Puebloans,
the Ancient Ones, the People.

We live close to the Earth and we know
the fire for how it warms us.

The water serpent hears our voices.
Water quenches our thirst.
Raindrops wash our skin, feed the corn in the fields,
and make the rocks shine.

The soil under our feet
is Mother to us and to our crops.

We breathe the invisible air.

The animals run
when they hear hunters coming
through the underbrush.

The hunters are men and boys.
They cross the ground silently in their moccasins,
eyes watching and ears listening.

The hunters do not want to scare the animals away.

When a kill is made—
a deer, an antelope, or a cottontail—
the hunters sing songs to the spirit of the animal.

They honor the animal they have killed
with their songs
because the animal died for them.

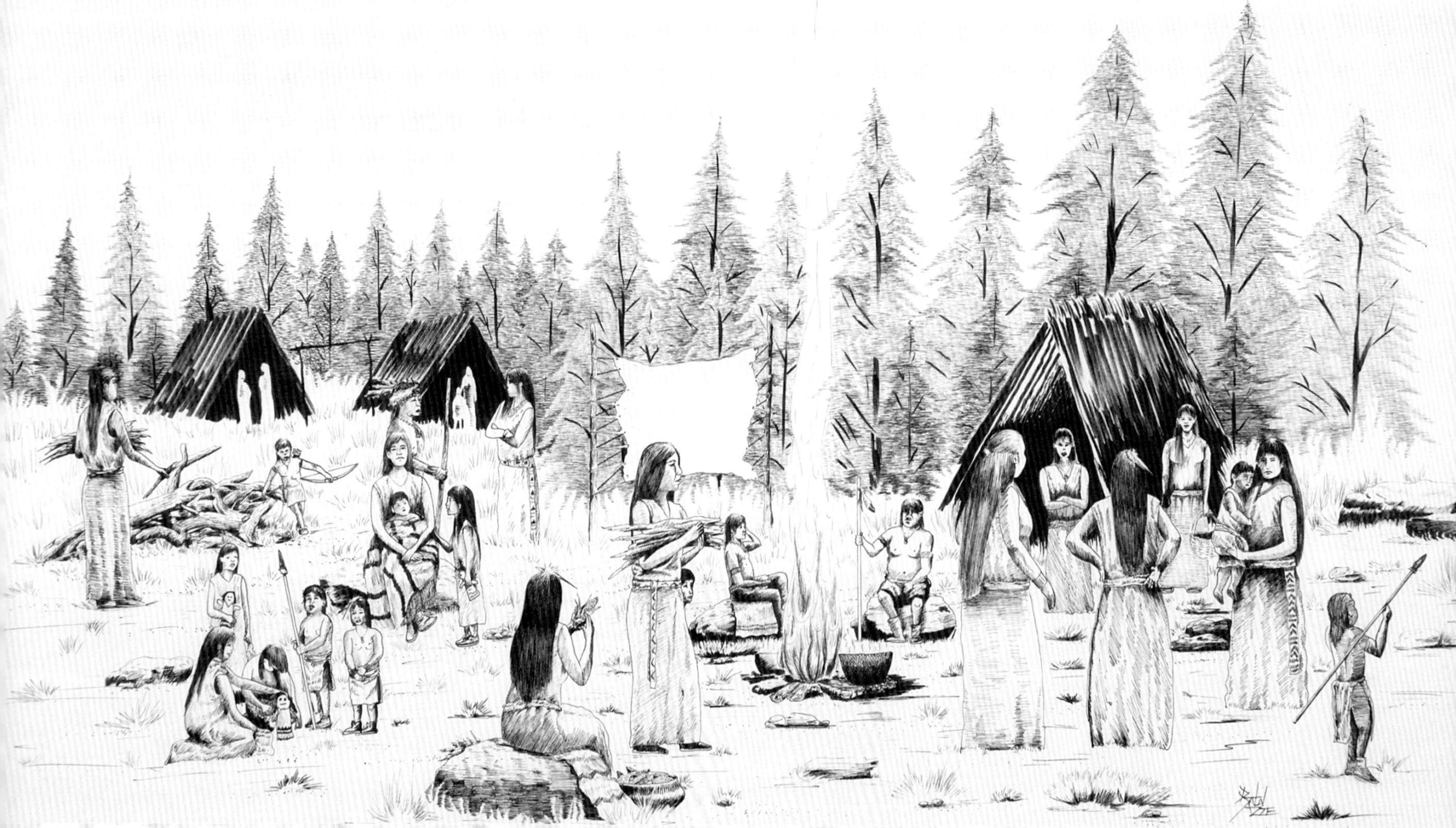

The day is ending and the sun is setting.

Women, young girls, babies,
and old people wait in the village.
They are eager to know what the men and boys
will bring back from the hunt.

Everyone is hungry.

The women are skilled with their blades.
They skin the animal the men bring home
and cut the meat into pieces
for all to share.

The older children,
boys and girls,
blow on embers to make
the fire flare up bright and warm.

All the People eat.

The dwellings of the People are warm
and the hunters are proud.

The women smile,
satisfied to see their children well fed.

It has been a good day.

There are times when the rains do not come
and there is no meat to cook.
The women keep busy
by sewing hides with bone needles.

These dry times are hard.
The water serpent does not hear
the voices of the People.

The women and girls forage for berries.

They drop seeds into the ground
and hope there will be enough rain
for the corn to grow.

Every day the People pray for rain.

Until the rains arrive
the People make do
with what little they have.

They often go hungry.

The children do not complain
because they know better.

In the fields the women and girls tend the corn.
The men sharpen their arrow points
and dream of the next hunt.

Still, no rain falls.

The men and boys travel
far from the village
in search of game.

Animals are hard to find.
They, too, are hungry and thirsty.

When thunderstorms build
over the mountains
and rush across the sky,
bolts of electric blue lightning strike,
and the People smile.

No matter how hard the times are,
the People do not look for a new home.

The shamans go to the rocks and pray for rain.
They make images of the water serpent
with their chipping stones.
They sing songs and tell the spirits
what they hunger for,
how thirsty they are.

The shamans are holy men and women.
They know what others cannot know—
how to talk to the spirits
with songs and pictures on stones.

The shamans etch images
and the spirits see
with their invisible eyes.

Boys and girls play flutes
to keep the shamans happy
while they work.

The women bring cornmeal and water.

The shamans make figures on the rocks
in the shapes of animals, corn,
thunderclouds, and raindrops.
They draw frogs and sheep and sometimes
water serpents and shooting stars.

The shamans are patient
and they work until their task is done.

"Here comes the rain!" shouts a boy.

The boy is happy. He dances in a circle.

The People are excited. The rains are back.

Now there will be plenty to eat,
corn ripening in the fields,
and deer gathering at the water holes.

There might even be a bobcat watching
from a secret hiding place.

Life for the People is the same as before.
The hunters crouch under piñon
and juniper pines, watching.

The hunters hide with their bows ready.

The women work as they always have,
tending the corn and the babies
and sewing hides.

There is enough to eat.

There is water to quench thirst
and warmth
from many glowing fires.